27 PRINCIPLES EVERY INVESTOR SHOULD KNOW

By Steven J. Atkinson | Illustrations by Dan Roam

Copyright © 2019 Buckingham Wealth Partners

All rights reserved. No part of this publication may be reproduced, distributed, or transmitted in any form or by any means without the prior written permission of the publisher, except in the case of brief quotations embodied in critical reviews and certain noncommercial uses permitted by copyright law.

IRN: R 19-018

Printed in the United States of America

First Printing: July 2019
Second Printing: January 2020

ISBN-13: 978-1-7332412-0-5

First Edition

Dedication

Each day, thousands of independent financial advisors navigate complex regulations, the unique challenges of business ownership, and an ever-changing digital landscape to help clients achieve their dreams.

As many families can attest, a great financial advisor is invaluable for so many reasons, many of which have nothing to do with money. From welcoming new grandkids and purchasing a home to layoffs and divorce, financial advisors are there every step of the way to provide support, encouragement, and financial stability.

Trusted financial advisors don't just pick stocks and rebalance accounts — their impact is much loftier: They help individuals feel confident about their decision to retire, they provide reassurance that children and grandchildren will be properly cared for when the time comes, they foster hope by finding creative solutions that help ordinary people turn dreams into a reality. Their work is of the utmost importance — a matter of security, stability, and legacy.

This book is dedicated to those hard-working advisors and their clients who dare to dream and take action toward making them a reality.

Foreword

We live in a world of abundant consumer choices, which can empower us but also create confusion, anxiety, and frustration.

Investing is no different. Investors in 2019 have access to more than 3,000 stocks in the U.S. and more than 10,000 stocks in the international markets. They also can choose from more than 10,000 mutual funds and exchange-traded funds (ETFs). In 2017, the U.S. Bureau of Labor Statistics estimated that more than 200,000 financial advisors offer their services in the U.S. Adding to the complexity are hundreds of financial publications, TV shows, online networks, and investment newsletters — all offering their versions of financial insight and advice.

How can one make sense of the jargon and competing messages?

"27 Principles Every Investor Should Know" cuts through the noise and helps individuals understand a complex subject through well-chosen concepts and clear explanations. The book embodies the art of simplicity at its best — easy to read and visually appealing yet grounded in sound principles that have emerged in the evolution of modern investing. It blends the hard tenets of the rigorous scientific research developed by leading academics in finance with the soft, behavioral side of investing.

Over the past century, the time required for information to reach investors has shortened from months, to weeks, to days, to hours, to minutes, to seconds, and arguably, to a microsecond. In this digital age, one may struggle to believe that an investor can consistently maintain a competitive advantage by having exclusive access to information impacting a stock, bond, or other publicly traded security. Furthermore, a vast group of economists — from Adam Smith to Nobel laureates such as F.A. Hayek, Milton Friedman, and Eugene Fama — have put forth theories and evidence supporting the notion that markets collectively know more than any single investor. Rather than trying to outguess markets, investors should accept prices as fair and focus on the factors they can control, such as diversifying across markets, balancing tradeoffs, managing costs, and applying discipline.

Many of the principles in this book are extensions of these concepts — beginning with the importance of having a specific, workable plan and the vital role financial advisors can play in the investment process. Investing is a lifelong journey. But to start that journey, you need to know where you are going, and an experienced guide can make all the difference. Education helps alleviate uncertainty — and the sharper the insights, the better you can understand investing fundamentals, manage your expectations, and stick with your plan through all kinds of markets.

"27 Principles Every Investor Should Know" will help people redefine their investment experience and become empowered investors.

Apollo Lupescu, PhD
Vice President, Dimensional Fund Advisors

Contents

Introduction	1
Successful Investing Starts With a Plan	3
Start Investing as Early as You Can	5
Invest for the Long Term	7
Investing Is Hard — Get Help From a Trusted Advisor	9
Know the Difference Between Advisors and Salespeople	11
Put Science and Academic Research on Your Side	13
Don't Try to Pick Individual Stocks	15
Don't Try to Predict Markets	17
Invest as if Markets Are Efficient	19
If You Can't Beat the Market, Own the Market	21
Past Performance Is No Indication of Future Results	23
Risk Is the Price of Admission to Investing	25
Understand How Risk and Return Are Related	27
Unnecessary Risks Are Unnecessary	29
Invest Globally	31
Retirement Success Depends More on Lower Volatility Than Higher Returns	33
Average Returns Can Be Misleading	35
Plan for Inflation	37
Your Behavior Can Impact Your Success	39
Don't Turn a Temporary Loss Into a Permanent Decline	41
Sometimes the Best Thing to Do Is Nothing	43
Invest Regularly: Disciplined Investors Catch Unexpected Opportunities	45
Plan for the Unexpected	47
Taxes Matter: Don't Pay More Than You Need To	49
Fees and Expenses Matter: Don't Pay More Than You Need To	51
Be an Investor, Not a Speculator	53
Have an Investment Philosophy and Stick to It	55

Introduction

Investing can sometimes feel a little overwhelming. It is such an important part of our lives, but not knowing where to turn for reliable information can be frustrating. What is noise, which should be avoided, and what is useful information, which should be implemented? Most of us want an approach that we can understand and believe in, which is based on research, analysis, and evidence — not luck or prognostication.

The good news is that in recent years, academic research has made enormous progress in understanding how to improve our chances of success as long-term investors. Unfortunately, the academic community doesn't necessarily do a good job educating investors. Research papers filled with charts and data are useful, but they are not always easy to follow. Fortunately, a group of financial advisors and investors have emerged over the past few decades to embrace academia over the traditional Wall Street methods.

The idea for this book started with us wanting to gather the plainspoken investing principles based off the academic research and put them in one place. We found there were countless ways investors are learning and leveraging these principles in the form of simple stories, sketches, and soundbites. That became the foundation for this book. Luckily, we've worked with some amazing investors and financial advisors who openly shared their ideas and "a-ha!" moments. We hope you will find an "a-ha" moment of your own while reading this book.

We believe that understanding and applying the 27 principles can help make you a more patient and — ultimately — successful long-term investor. We hope they will empower you to understand the difference between the noise (not useful information for your personal goals) and the science (relevant information for your personal goals).

This book is for all the ordinary people who have dedicated their lives to working and saving in order to achieve important goals, such as providing for children's education and enjoying a secure retirement. Life is complicated. Investing shouldn't be.

Principle 1:
Successful Investing Starts With a Plan

"If you fail to plan, you are planning to fail."
— Benjamin Franklin, Founding Father

Many think investing is simply about making smart investments and getting good returns, but it is critical to have a plan in place beforehand to ensure that you know WHY you are investing. This plan, which is built in close collaboration with your financial advisor, should reflect what is most important to you — your values, needs, concerns, and hopes.

It is similar to building a new house. Initially, you meet with an architect to share what you are looking for. Your architect will ask a lot of questions to make sure he or she understands your preferences and has a good feel for your vision.

Your architect will then put together a blueprint for your dream house, and you can start construction. There will be some changes along the way, but without this blueprint, your dream home could become a nightmare.

Financial planning works the same way. Your financial advisor will help clarify your goals and dreams for the future, focusing on key life areas such as helping and protecting your family and building a legacy. Your advisor will then create a plan that is both specific and unique to your situation, and then put together a portfolio to make this plan possible.

Because life changes along the way, you should meet regularly with your advisor to ensure that the plan is still on track and that your circumstances or goals have not changed.

INVEST EARLY.

Principle 2:
Start Investing as Early as You Can

"The best time to plant a tree is 20 years ago. The second best time is now."
— African Proverb

When it comes to retirement, time really is money. While the amount you can expect to receive from Social Security will vary depending upon your income, the reality is that Social Security will replace only about 35%-40% of your income. Even your savings might not be enough, since we are living longer. If you're in good health when you retire, there's a good chance you'll live well into your 80s and beyond. It's possible that you will be retired for 30 years — almost as long as you worked!

So, the sooner you invest, the longer your money has to grow. Even a few extra years can make a big difference.

Consider two investors: Investor A, a 21-year-old, saves $100 a month for nine years and then stops at age 30, for a total contribution of $10,800. Investor B saves $100 a month from age 30 to age 65 (35 years), for a total contribution of $42,000. Assuming an 8% rate of return, Investor A is able to retire at 65, with $231,047, while Investor B retires with $215,635.[1]

Just think how much further ahead Investor A would be if he'd kept investing right up until retirement, or had been able to save more than $100 a month.

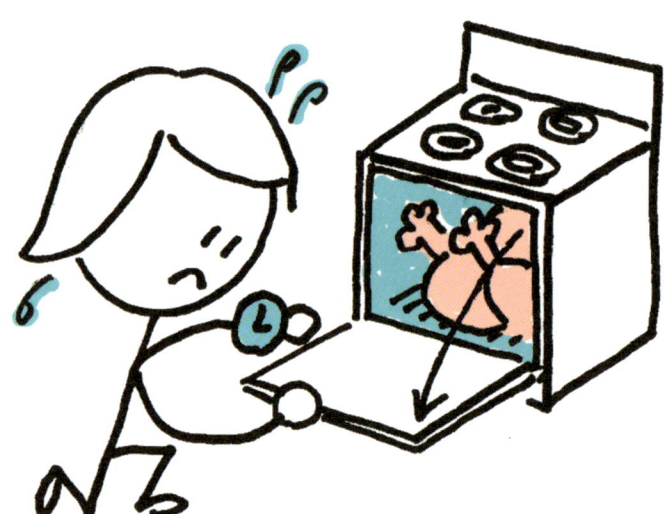

TRUST THE PROCESS.

Principle 3:
Invest for the Long Term

"All good things arrive unto them that wait — and don't die in the meantime."
— Mark Twain, Author

Over the last nine decades, the U.S. experienced nine bear markets and 15 recessions or depressions, World War II and the Vietnam War, and any number of crises big and small.

Yet markets have shown a remarkable ability to reward patient, long-term investors for staying invested. This is important, since most of us are investing for the long term, for a retirement that could last as long as three decades (or even longer).

We must keep this long-term horizon in perspective when judging the success of our portfolio and the financial plan it supports. It is like cooking a turkey for Thanksgiving. Because a 20-pound turkey requires four to five hours to cook, we do not measure success by opening the oven every few minutes to see how things are going. Instead, we give the oven time to work, checking only periodically to make sure everything is on track (and to make any necessary adjustments).

When it comes to your portfolio, don't judge success on a quarterly or even annual basis. Instead, focus on how you are progressing toward your goals, including any life changes that may impact those goals. This helps you to stay focused and prevents short-term market fluctuations from compromising your future. Trust the process and your plan, and don't open the oven all the time. That way, there is only one turkey involved.

Principle 4:
Investing Is Hard — Get Help From a Trusted Advisor

"It is not enough for a professional to be right: An advisor's job is to be helpful."
— David H. Maister, Professor

Some things are just too difficult or stressful to do on your own. Like a dietitian or a personal trainer, a financial advisor can help set up the right plan for you, then monitor and motivate you so you end up with the results you want.

There are four key benefits to working with an advisor:

Competence: providing the critical things that help drive successful long-term outcomes, including planning, asset allocation, rebalancing, and working with other financial professionals.

Coaching: providing education and guidance through the emotions of investing, which can cause us to compromise long-term goals.

Convenience: delegating the complex and time-consuming work of investing and planning to your advisor.

Continuity: having someone who knows your wishes and goals and can preserve your legacy and protect those you care most about if anything happens to you.

Remember, choosing a financial advisor is one of the most important decisions you can make.

Principle 5:
Know the Difference Between Advisors and Salespeople

"Are you willing to sell a person a shoe that doesn't fit vs. losing the sale because you don't have the right size?"
— David Booth, Founder of Dimensional Fund Advisors

Unfortunately, too many financial firms and their employees focus more on selling products versus trying to provide advice and solve investor needs. Only independent financial advisors are legally required to act as fiduciaries — which means they must always put your interests as a client ahead of their own. In addition, they must disclose all important information to you, including fees and any conflicts of interest.

So when independent advisors make a recommendation, it has to be in your best interests — not because they want to make a quick sale. It is like the difference between getting health advice from a doctor versus a pharmaceutical salesperson. Pharmaceutical sales reps can only sell the medicine their company manufactures. A doctor, on the other hand, must prescribe the right medicine for each patient, regardless of the manufacturer. Independent advisors take the same approach when advising their clients. They are indifferent to who makes a financial product; their only focus is getting the best resources to help solve each person's unique situation.

Principle 6:
Put Science and Academic Research on Your Side

"The important thing in science is not so much to obtain new facts as to discover new ways of thinking about them."

— Sir William Bragg, Scientist

Many of us want to be in better shape and live a healthy lifestyle — but we wish it were easier. The health and fitness industry understands this perfectly. They bombard us with advertisements about how easy it is to lose weight and get in shape.

Alternatively, consider the evidence-based approach the medical community has developed for weight loss and healthy living. It might not be exactly what we want to hear (eat sensibly – exercise more) but at least we have a path to success to follow if we choose. This evidence-based approach increases our probability of success, and we don't have to waste time and money on solutions that don't work!

As with the fitness industry, there is no magic pill for successful investing. Cable financial news networks and financial magazines hype stories on "How to Pick the Best Stocks Now" or "Why You Need to Own This Company." Sadly, these ideas rarely work.

The good news for investors is that there are evidence-based investment strategies, grounded in academic research, that may increase potential return and decrease potential risk. Sound advice may not sell magazines or drive TV ratings, but it can do something much more important: increase your probability of reaching your financial goals.

Principle 7:
Don't Try to Pick Individual Stocks

"One of the funniest things about the stock market is that every time one man buys, another sells, and both think they are astute."
— William Feather, Author

If you've ever watched a flock of birds or school of fish, you've seen how they move in unison, changing directions quickly and precisely, all together.

But if you focus on just one fish (or bird), things get much more random. The animal might be slightly out of sync. It might go left when the school goes right. It might lag or straggle.

It is much easier to see what the group is doing and where it is headed.

Stocks are the same way. Individual companies may or may not follow what the rest of the market is doing. Perhaps their CEO was just fired. Perhaps a new product isn't selling well. Therefore, investing in an individual company is much riskier than investing in the market as a whole. It is also really difficult to pick stocks that will do better than the market — that will swim ahead. But over time the market as a whole tends to move in predictable directions and reward investors who swim with the current, and not against it.

Principle 8:
Don't Try to Predict Markets

"It would be wonderful if we could avoid the setbacks with timely exits, but nobody has figured out how to predict them."

— Peter Lynch, Money Manager

Wall Street and the popular financial press want you to believe that in order to make money in the stock market, you need to invest based on what's about to happen. That's the message sent out every day by market strategists, brokers, analysts, mutual fund managers, and the media — predict the future accurately, and you'll score big.

In truth, no one can accurately forecast market movements on a consistent basis. Why? Because we're talking about the future, and the future is, by its very nature, uncertain. We cannot predict with absolute confidence the direction of the economy, stock prices, or events that will have an impact on the markets.

Consider this one notable example (of many). At the beginning of 2008, right before the beginning of the Great Recession, all the major firms on Wall Street were predicting up markets for the year. As we now know, their predictions were disastrously wrong.

The upshot: Even the brightest analysts, the most highly regarded money managers in the world, or the most plugged-in and well-respected financial publications can seldom tell you what's going to happen next, let alone give you reliable advice on how to position your investments to take advantage. That doesn't mean that a fund manager, a talking head on cable financial news networks, or the guy who walks his dog down your street every morning won't sometimes get it right. They will. The credit, however, usually goes to luck — not skill. And your financial future is too important to leave to chance.

Principle 9:
Invest as if Markets Are Efficient

"[T]hose who disagree with market efficiency simply assert that it stands to common sense that greater effort to get facts and greater acumen in analyzing those facts will pay off in better performance.... By this logic, a cure for cancer must have been found by 1955."

— Paul Samuelson, Winner of the Nobel Memorial Prize in Economic Sciences

At a neighbor's garage sale, you notice there is a Babe Ruth rookie baseball card on sale, priced at 25 cents. Obviously, your neighbor is not a big baseball fan, since this card is worth tens of thousands of dollars.

Just as you are about to hand over a quarter, another neighbor walks up. She also knows the value of the card is way more than 25 cents and offers $5. Pretty soon, you and your neighbor are having a bidding war, until the price you pay for the card is close to its actual value. And it only took one additional participant to get there.

Financial markets work similarly on a larger scale, with millions of investors buying and selling securities each day to determine fair market value.

Because markets usually do a good job incorporating all publicly known information into prices, investors are better off acting as if current prices are correct instead of trying to guess their future direction. This also allows you to focus on your overall plan instead of trying to predict how markets will react to headlines.

Principle 10:
If You Can't Beat the Market, Own the Market

"Very few investors manage to beat the market. But in an astonishing triumph of hope over experience, millions of investors keep trying."
— Jonathan Clements, Author

It isn't easy to beat the stock market. In fact, most money managers typically underperform. And those who are able to beat the market one year struggle to stay on top in subsequent years.

Why? Turns out that outperforming the market may be more about luck than skill. Imagine a baseball stadium filled with 20,000 fans. You give each fan a quarter and ask them to flip it at the same time. Heads they can stay, tails they must leave the stadium. Because the odds of heads or tails are 50-50, after the first flip about 10,000 fans will stay and 10,000 will leave. The remaining fans flip again and 5,000 stay and 5,000 leave.

After a total of 14 flips, the odds are that only one person will be left, having managed to flip 14 heads in a row. Now fill the arena back up. Would you expect the same person to flip 14 heads in a row? Probably not. A great stock picker is like a great quarter flipper. It's mostly about luck. In fact, studies have found that active managers as a group do worse than random chance. Meaning they might actually improve their stock-picking performance if they used coin flips to make stock picks.

Since trying to beat the market leads to a high probability of underperformance, most investors would be better off simply just owning the market.

Principle 11:
Past Performance Is No Indication of Future Results

"Events in the past may be roughly divided into those which probably never happened and those which do not matter."

— William Ralph Inge, Author

You need to get to the airport, and you are not sure how long it will take. You call a friend, and she says it takes 30 minutes to two hours. That's somewhat useful, but it is a wide range, and it is based on past performance. You need more current information so you don't miss your flight.

That's when you open a mapping app that uses the latest traffic and weather conditions to let you know almost exactly how long it will take to get to the airport right now.

Investing is similar. The past is a good rough guide. It gives you a range of what you can expect. Stocks will generally outperform bonds over the long term. International stocks are usually riskier than U.S. stocks. And so on. But if you rely only on the past, you might be led astray. It is like driving forward while looking backward.

Instead, using the most current information typically leads to more sensible decisions. Not what the market did or will do, but what is happening right now. This is what smart money managers do every day. And it gives you a much better chance of getting where you want to go with fewer surprises.

Principle 12:
Risk Is the Price of Admission to Investing

"Everything in life, individually or socially, is a trade-off. We determine the risk levels we're willing to tolerate."
— Robert Merton, Winner of the Nobel Memorial Prize in Economic Sciences

The fact is simply this: Where there is no risk, there is little reward, which is why it is so hard to make much money on a "sure" thing.

Stock markets that always rewarded investors or, conversely, never made anyone money would quickly collapse. Only a market that has both up and down periods offers the potential for long-term returns. While we can't predict when these ups and downs will occur, we do know — in general — that markets rise and fall for rational reasons — strong or weak economies, geopolitical issues, new technologies, etc. One of your major decisions as an investor is how much risk you can tolerate. Which in turn determines how much potential return you might expect.

Investing in stocks is investing in thousands of companies that have created something the economy finds valuable. Those companies that survive and thrive are innovating over time, developing or acquiring the expertise to bring newer and better products to market. Not every company will survive, and markets as a whole will still go up and down. But if you can handle the risk, you will probably be rewarded over the long term for staying the course.

Potential: 100 pts

Potential: 2 pts

To get more points, you have to take more <u>risks</u>.

Principle 13:
Understand How Risk and Return Are Related

"Yes, risk-taking is error prone, otherwise it would be called sure-thing-taking."
— Jim McMahon, Football Player

Imagine you are a competitive diver in the Olympics. You will be judged on your form, your technique, and the difficulty of your dives. The more complicated a dive, the higher your potential score. But also, the higher the chances of not executing the dive perfectly.

Investing is similar. The more risk you take on in your portfolio, the greater your expected return potential. Academic research has shown that different stocks have different expected returns. For example, small company and value company stocks have greater expected returns — and risks — than growth and large company stocks.

Why? Let's say you wanted to invest in a tech company. You narrow your options down to two. Joe's Tech is a small company, newly listed on the stock exchange. They have a lot of innovative ideas and hope to become a great business. They also aren't generating a profit yet and have substantial debt. The other company is one of the largest in the world — Apple. They have strong financial statements, impressive sales, extensive research budgets, and a strong product pipeline. If the returns of these stocks were expected to be the same, no one would invest in a lesser-known and riskier company like Joe's Tech. The reason smaller companies can attract investors is because of their higher expected return (versus an established company) if they achieve their ambitious goals. They might become the next Apple. They also might go out of business. This is the risk, but also the potential reward.

STAY IN THE CENTER!

Principle 14:
Unnecessary Risks Are Unnecessary

"Diversification is the only free lunch in finance."
— Dr. Harry Markowitz, Winner of the Nobel Memorial Prize in Economic Sciences

The Golden Gate Bridge in San Francisco is one of the most beautiful and iconic bridges in the world. It is also a good way to think about your pathway to retirement — from the hustle and bustle of the city (work) to the calm, rolling hills (retirement).

But first you have to cross the bridge. Seems easy enough. But what if they removed the guardrails? Where would you drive? Along the edges, with nothing to stop you from plummeting into the waters below? Or right down the middle?

When it comes to your retirement portfolio, you drive down the middle of the bridge with a broadly diversified portfolio that holds thousands of companies around the world.

The less diversified you are, the closer you will get to the edge of the bridge. Sometimes, this could mean higher returns, but it also might mean greater losses.

With a globally diversified portfolio, you won't be the single best performer in any period, but you will also have fewer reasons to worry about poor returns from a single asset class. And that keeps your portfolio in the center of the bridge as you head toward retirement.

For most of us, whether we are crossing a bridge or investing, we want to follow a safer path. Our future is too important to risk.

THE WHOLE WORLD LOVES CHOCOLATE CHIPS!
Thank you Switzerland!

Principle 15:
Invest Globally

"Nothing is more expensive than a missed opportunity."
— H. Jackson Brown, Jr., Author

For many of us, the smell of a fresh batch of chocolate chip cookies brings back happy memories of childhood. Often, the chocolate chips were Nestlé Toll House®. Chocolate chip cookies may be an American invention, but Nestlé is actually a Swiss company — though their products have been sold in America and have been a part of our everyday life for a very long time. Perhaps you bought your baking supplies at Trader Joe's, which is owned by a German company. And baked them in an oven made by Korean-owned Samsung.

As investors, it is important to realize that many of the companies we buy products from on a daily basis are headquartered all over the world. We don't limit our consumption to U.S. products, so why would we limit our investment portfolios to U.S. companies? Instead, it makes sense to invest in many of the great companies of America and the rest of the world to maximize the potential of our portfolio.

We like to think of the U.S. as a world leader, but over the past several decades, America has never been the #1 market in the world in annualized performance. Nobody knows what the future will bring. But if you own many companies around the world, you can worry less if any one company or even one country experiences losses. Keep in mind that international stocks can be riskier than U.S. stocks due to currency and political risks, among others. This is why it is so important for you to carefully decide how to allocate your portfolio between U.S. and international stocks.

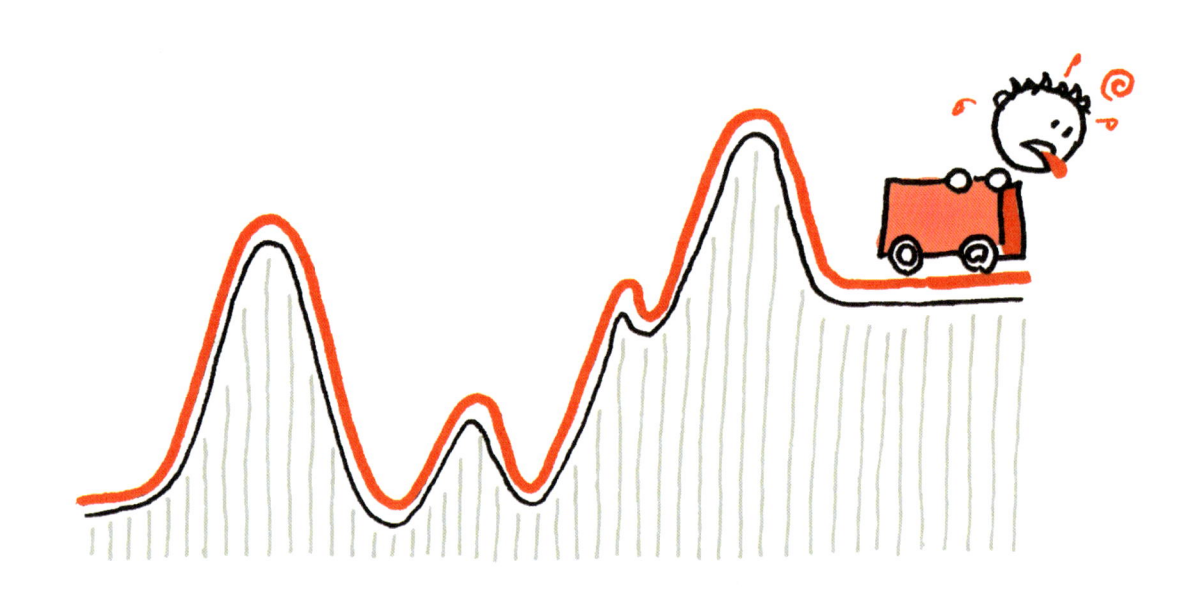

Which would you rather ride?

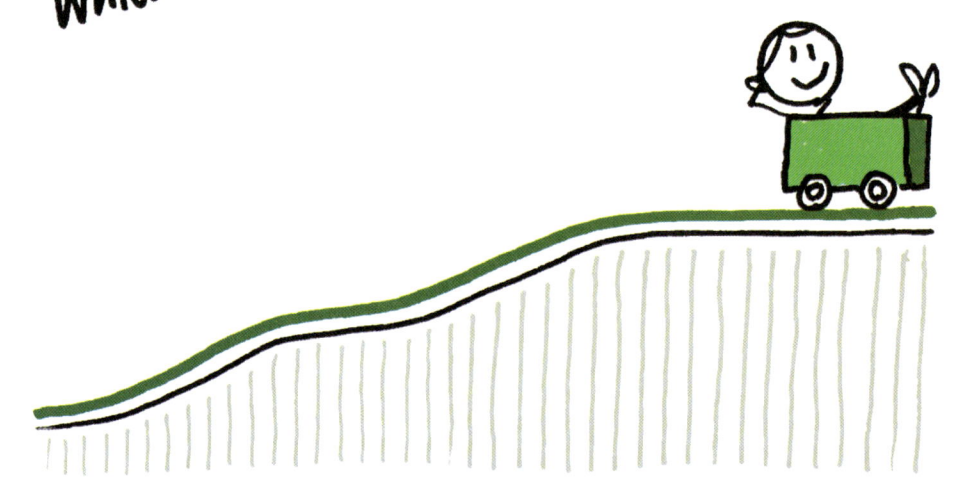

Principle 16:
Retirement Success Depends More on Lower Volatility Than Higher Returns

"Fragility is the quality of things that are vulnerable to volatility."

— Nassim Nicholas Taleb, Author and Statistician

If you've been invested since 2000, you've certainly lived through more than your share of excitement: two bear markets, the Great Recession, war, terrorism, and some of the worst days in the history of the stock market!

All these events led to extremely volatile markets. No one likes volatility, but if you are in retirement taking money out of your portfolio, volatility can compromise your long-term success. Think of it like riding rollercoasters at the amusement park. If you were going to be on for a long time, would you rather ride the big, exciting rollercoaster? Or the kiddie rollercoaster?

Lowering volatility is important for investors, especially those making regular withdrawals, because it can help keep your money working for you longer. And that can make a big difference in retirement when every dollar counts.

Your financial advisor can put together a portfolio that helps minimize volatility in retirement and increases the odds of not outliving your money.

Different climates.

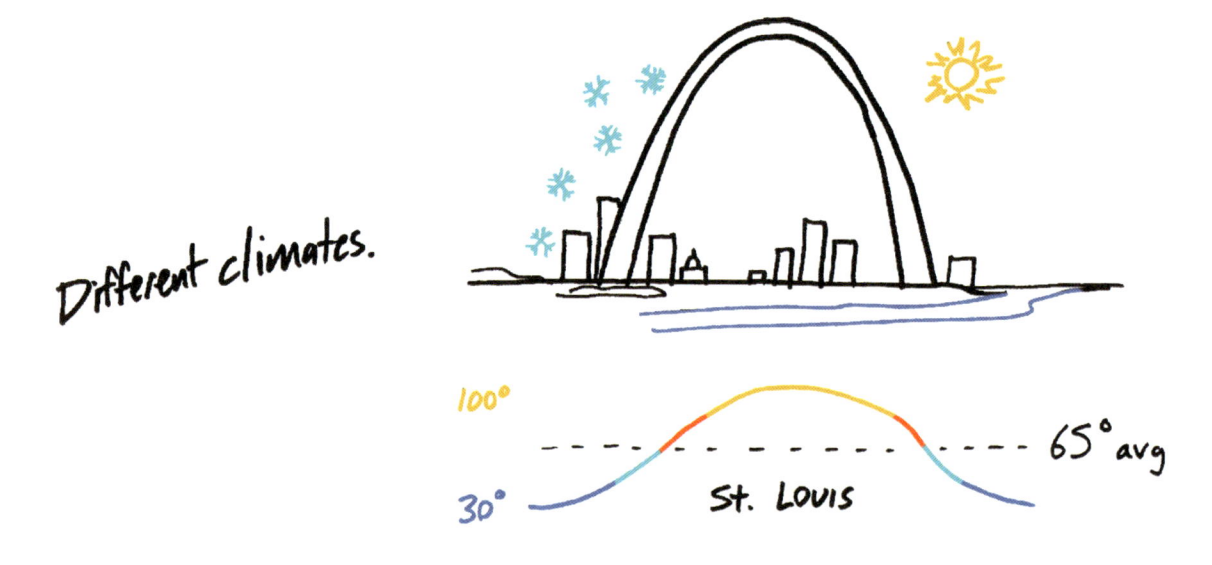

100°
30° 65° avg
St. Louis

Same *average* temperature.

100°
30° 65° avg
SAN FRANCISCO

Principle 17:
Average Returns Can Be Misleading

"I abhor averages . . . A man may have six meals one day and none the next, making an average of three meals per day, but that is not a good way to live."
— Louis D. Brandeis, Supreme Court Justice

You are looking to retire somewhere with a mild climate. So you do a little research and find two cities that have an annual average temperature of about 65 degrees: San Francisco and St. Louis.

But then you do a little more research and find that while San Francisco is pretty much 65 degrees most of the year, St. Louis has hot summers and cold winters — something you would never know just looking at the averages. Similarly, many investors make the mistake of focusing only on average rates of return — sometimes with disastrous consequences.

Consider the S&P 500. Over the last nine decades, it has had up years and down years, but there were just a handful of years when the annual return came close to the average return. And this can be challenging for some investors to handle.

This is why it makes sense to work with a financial advisor who uses tools that account for variability in returns. Good planning is an ongoing and dynamic process between you and your advisor, which helps minimize uncertainty and maximize your potential for future success.

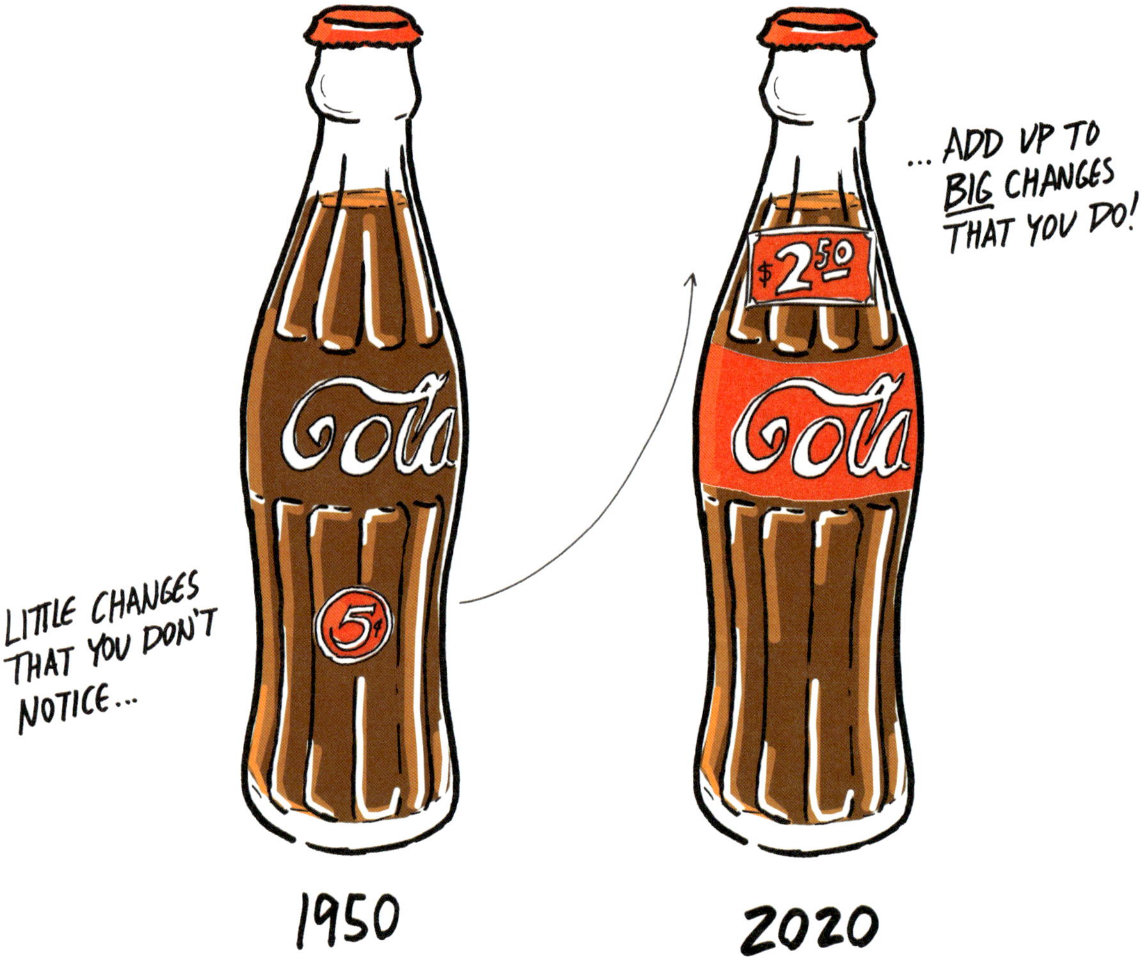
LITTLE CHANGES THAT YOU DON'T NOTICE...
... ADD UP TO BIG CHANGES THAT YOU DO!
Cola
5¢
Cola
$2.50
1950
2020

Principle 18:
Plan for Inflation

"Inflation is taxation without legislation."
— Milton Friedman, Winner of the Nobel Memorial Prize in Economic Sciences

A typical 65-year-old baby boomer couple has a joint life expectancy of 30 years, meaning there is a high probability that at least one of them is going to live to age 95. And 30 years is a very long time to plan for. Think of your own life and where you were 30 years ago and all that has happened since . . . changes in career, family, where you live, and how. Think what it may mean to spend a similar amount of time in retirement.

Many of us do a pretty good job saving and investing, but we can overlook one of the great dangers to a secure retirement — inflation. Historically, inflation has averaged around 3%. Doesn't sound like much, but over time, the impact can be substantial. A 3% inflation rate means that $1 this year will be worth 97 cents next year. In 10 years, $1 will be worth 73 cents. In 30 years, $1 will be worth just 41 cents. This means $100,000 in the bank today could be worth just $41,000 in 30 years.

If your nest egg isn't keeping up with inflation, your money is disappearing without you even realizing it! And while inflation is cutting your purchasing power, it is also making many things more expensive. Think of a bottle of Coke that used to cost 75 cents 30 years ago and is now more than $1.50. Or a gallon of milk that was $2.50 and is now $3.50. And prices of some things such as education, health care, and housing have actually increased significantly faster than the overall rate of inflation.

The corrosive impact of inflation is one of the primary reasons we invest. Each year, inflation eats away at all we've earned and saved, while stock markets offer us significant opportunities to grow our wealth.

BUY!!

REPEAT UNTIL BROKE...

SELL!!

YOUR EMOTIONS ARE <u>NOT</u> YOUR INVESTMENT STRATEGY.

Principle 19:
Your Behavior Can Impact Your Success

"The dominant determinants of long-term, real-life, investment returns are not market behavior, but investment behavior."

— Nick Murray, Author

For most of us, money is bound up with powerful emotions, such as security, confidence, and even, sometimes, fear. But the emotions of investing can cause us to lose focus on important areas of our life, most of which have absolutely nothing to do with the stock market.

We know that remaining patient and disciplined can be extremely difficult, especially when markets are soaring or plummeting. The way our brains are hardwired can cause us to make emotional decisions about our money at precisely the wrong moments: We "buy high" and "sell low."

Markets are prone to sharp and erratic movements, which can cause investors to sell at inopportune times. Conversely, during a strong bull market, investors often rush into the market because they feel elated and buy at the peak. Ultimately, this kind of emotional, short-term behavior can compromise your portfolio and your financial plan.

DON'T LEAVE THE MOVIE
JUST BECAUSE IT GETS SCARY.

Principle 20:
Don't Turn a Temporary Loss Into a Permanent Decline

"It is a rough road that leads to the heights of greatness."

— Seneca, Philosopher

Imagine there was an electronic sign on your home that always showed its latest price, or that you logged in to Zillow every day to check your home's valuation. If your home dropped in value by 15%, would you immediately sell it?

Probably not. Our house has a necessary functional value — even if the price goes down, we still need a place to live. The same may be true for investing. Its necessary functional value is to help us achieve our most important goals: educating kids, staying ahead of inflation, and enjoying a long and secure retirement.

When markets are open, stock prices change every second. Though markets have historically gone up over the long term, in the shorter term, prices can swing wildly and even decline severely.

This can lead some investors to panic and sell, turning a temporary decline into a permanent loss (since you no longer own the investments and can't benefit from any future rebound). It is a little like leaving a great movie just because there is a scary scene in the middle.

So the next time your portfolio value drops, ask yourself if it's worth creating a permanent loss or whether your reasons for investing in the first place (e.g., retirement) still apply.

KEEP CALM AND LET YOUR $$$ WORK

Principle 21:
Sometimes the Best Thing to Do Is Nothing

"Your money is like soap. The more you handle it the less you will have."
— Gene Fama Jr., Economist

You're in a hurry, but you're stuck in traffic. It seems like the lane you're in just isn't moving. But the cars in the next lane keep passing you. You're too smart to just sit there, so you change lanes only to find that now the lane you were just in is moving and you're stuck again. As you keep changing lanes, you realize you're actually going slower and get more frustrated.

Unfortunately, too many investors are impatient and keep changing lanes and finding themselves getting further behind. And this can be costly. On average, investors tend to significantly underperform the stock and bond markets.

Some might think they know when to buy and sell. But this means they have to be right twice: picking the best time to get in and out of the market. Few investors, even brilliant hedge fund managers, have done that predictably and consistently.

Other investors give in to panic or even greed and make hasty, emotional decisions. The objective advice and guidance of a financial advisor can help keep you on track and stop you from making hasty decisions that could crash your portfolio.

TO MAKE A CATCH, YOU NEED A LINE IN THE WATER.

Principle 22:
Invest Regularly: Disciplined Investors Catch Unexpected Opportunities

"There is no security on this earth; there is only opportunity."
— Douglas MacArthur, General

If you are a fisherman, you know there will be days when the fish aren't biting and other days when they take the bait the moment your line hits the water. But on good days or bad days, you will catch fish only if you are actually fishing.

This lesson is lost on many investors who try to pick and choose when to invest and when not to. They believe that if they can figure out the right times to be in the market (or out) they will make more money — and avoid steep declines.

Sounds good in theory. But the reality is that predicting the best and worst times to invest is difficult.

Consider that the third-best one-day return in the last three decades occurred only two days after the worst one-day return (stock market crash of 1987). Most investors who bailed out of the markets in response to the crash most likely missed a significant bounce-back.

Over the last 20 years, if you'd invested $100,000 in the S&P 500 and missed the 10 best days, your portfolio would have grown to $200,030.[2] However, if you'd stayed invested and "kept fishing," your portfolio would have grown to $400,135. Quite a catch!

BE PREPARED
FOR RAINY
DAYS!

Principle 23:
Plan for the Unexpected

"The shortest period of time lies between the minute you put some money away for a rainy day and the unexpected arrival of rain."
— Jane Bryant Quinn, Journalist

As you are packing for a trip to another city, you prudently decide to check the 10-day weather forecast there. If it will be cold, you pack a heavy coat. If it is supposed to rain, you bring an umbrella. You want to be prepared. Similarly, you want a financial plan that anticipates the unexpected.

First, you need to plan for sudden, unanticipated expenses, such as home repairs, medical bills, or losing a job. Many experts recommend you have at least three to six months' living expenses saved away and readily accessible for any "surprises" that come your way. In addition, be wary of financial products that make it hard for you to access your money if you need it unexpectedly.

Second, make sure you and your loved ones are properly protected. Depending on your situation, this can include everything from home and car insurance to long-term care and life insurance.

Third, make sure your plan factors in down markets. A well-diversified portfolio built around your comfort with risk can account for and help mitigate some of the impact of market declines.

Rainy days will happen. But the right long-term plan can keep you covered.

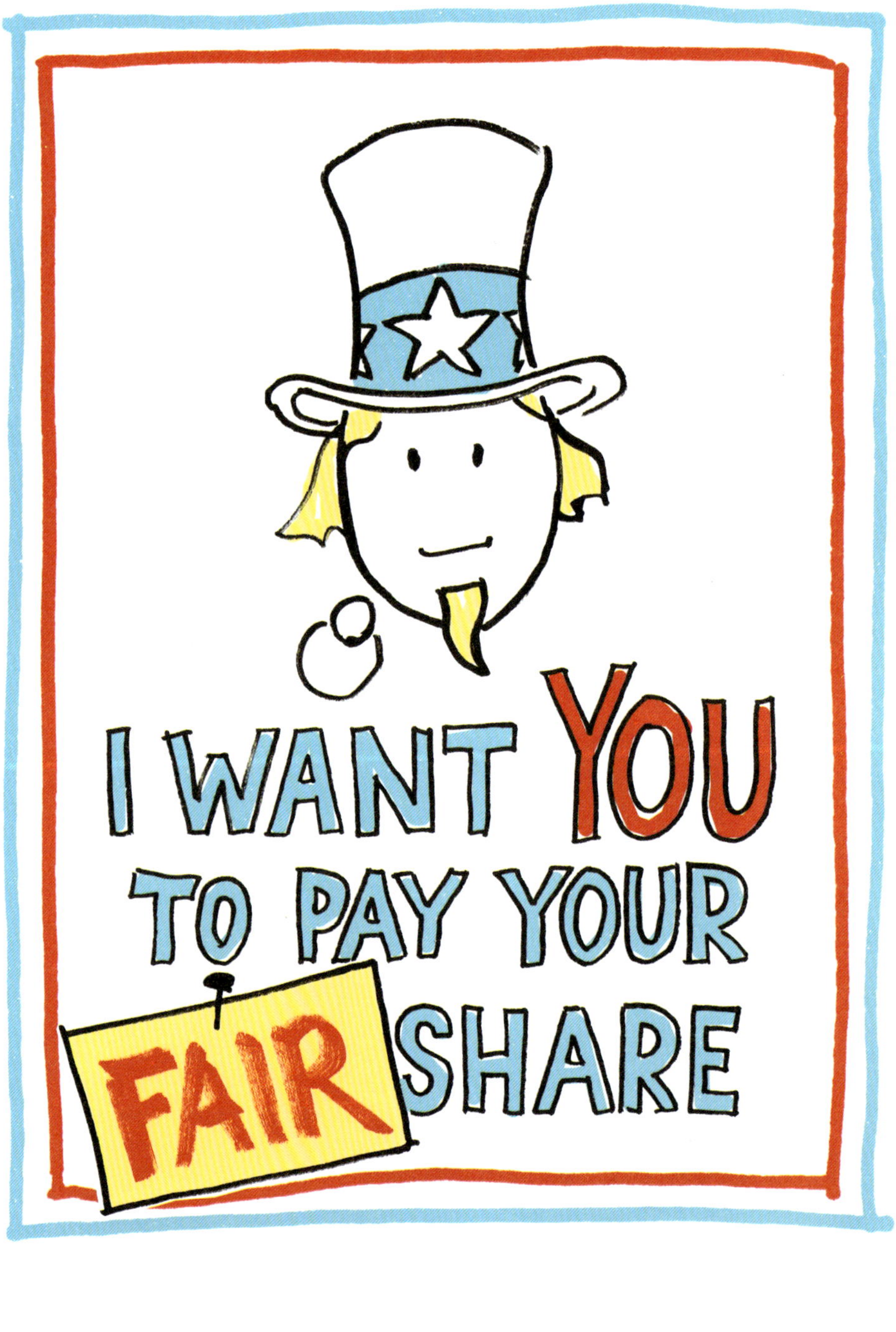
I WANT YOU
TO PAY YOUR
FAIR SHARE

Principle 24:
Taxes Matter: Don't Pay More Than You Need To

"I'm proud to pay taxes . . . the only thing is, I could be just as proud for half the money."
— Arthur Godfrey, Entertainer

Taxes help make possible many good things in society, but few of us want to pay the government more than our fair share . . . especially by accident. Investment mistakes can cost you unnecessary taxes, but there are several areas where smart tax strategies can make a big difference.

Tax-loss harvesting involves selling securities, usually at year-end, to realize portfolio losses, which you can use to offset any capital gains in your portfolio and therefore lower personal tax liability.

What you are invested in can also have a tax impact. The portfolio turnover and trading volume of many active mutual funds can result in more capital gains taxes than index or asset class funds.

Finally, asset location is a tax minimization strategy that is based on the different tax treatments of various types of investments. Using this strategy, an investor determines which securities should be held in tax-deferred accounts and which securities should be held in taxable accounts in order to maximize after-tax returns.

Everyone's situation is different, and tax minimization is something you should consult with your financial advisor on.

$5

$50

Principle 25:

Fees and Expenses Matter: Don't Pay More Than You Need To

"When you know the impact of little expenses, you will realize that there is nothing little in this world."
— Manoj Arora, Author

If you've ever ordered room service at a fancy hotel, you know that your club sandwich and soda will be marked up significantly from what you'd pay at the deli down the street. Many investment products are similarly marked up. And unlike an expensive sandwich, unnecessary investment costs can significantly eat into your returns over time.

That's not all: A 2016 study by Morningstar found that costs are the number one determinant of future performance. The higher the cost of an investment, the less likely it is to outperform its peers. And as the complexities of investments rise, so do their costs. Hedge funds, for example, typically charge 2% as well as 20% of any profits.

Mutual funds, especially those that are actively managed, also have a number of fees and expenses that can really add up. In fact, active funds are typically at least twice as expensive as index or asset class funds and generally don't perform as well. This is why it is so important to read the prospectus carefully for any product you are considering and understand exactly how much you are paying. Investing isn't free, but it doesn't have to be overpriced.

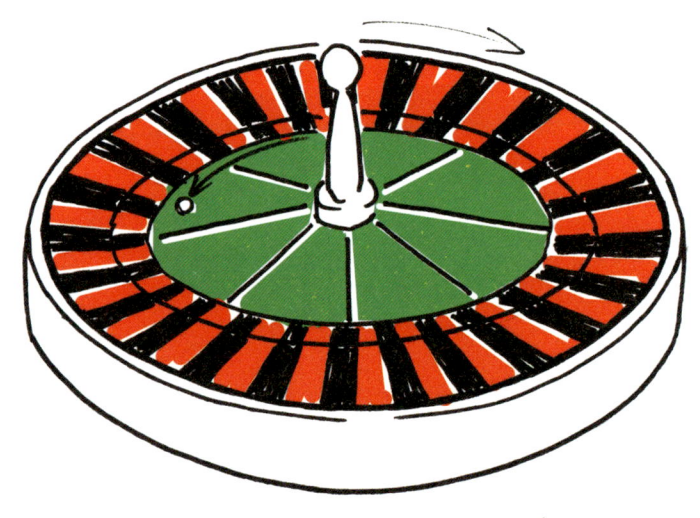

HOPING FOR A RETURN.

Vs.

EXPECTING A RETURN.

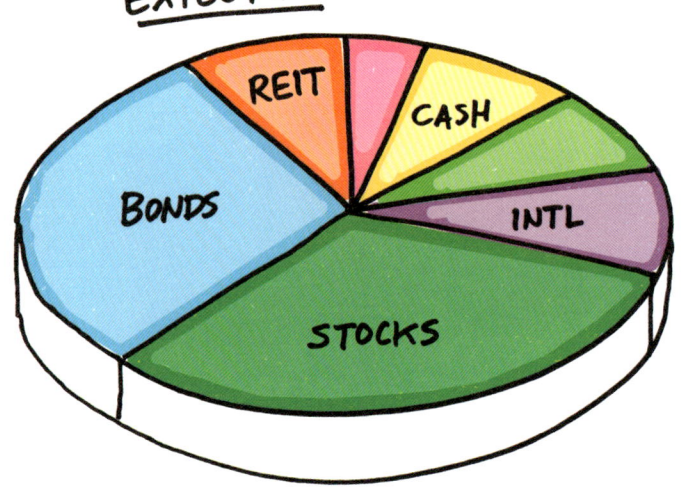

Principle 26:

Be an Investor, Not a Speculator

"Investing is expecting positive returns whereas speculating is hoping for positive returns."
— Eugene Fama Sr., Winner of the Nobel Memorial Prize in Economic Sciences

Understanding the difference between investing and speculating can make a significant difference when it comes to growing your money over time. Casinos know this difference well — it's the foundation of most of their profits.

Any casino game has two parties: the speculator or "gambler" and the house or "investor." Both play the game, but only one is truly investing. Why? It comes down to the odds. At best, gamblers have a 47% chance of winning. They can do little more than hope for a positive outcome. The casino, on the other hand, knows better. They know the odds are in their favor. If they stay disciplined, they win.

Unfortunately, most investors are actually speculating when they think they are investing. They hope for great returns by trying to predict the stock market or find the latest hot stock. These are NOT proven strategies for success, yet people try them every day.

The key to investing is to act like the casino, not the gambler. Diversify across thousands of securities. And don't try to predict markets (or the next hand). Over the long term, history has shown that these behaviors may improve your odds of success.

BELIEVE IN WHERE YOU ARE GOING.

Principle 27:
Have an Investment Philosophy and Stick to It

"The important thing about an investment philosophy is that you have one you can stick with."

— David Booth, Founder of Dimensional Fund Advisors

You decide to go on a long cross-country hike to a beautiful mountain lake. It will take you a couple of days, and the path will be steep and wind through forests and fields. Before setting off, most of us would get the right gear together, make sure we have enough food, and carefully map our route. We wouldn't put a bunch of random things in our backpack and just head off in the general direction of the lake.

Unfortunately, too many investors invest precisely this way, gathering investments together without a plan or purpose beyond hoping for good returns. Generally, they are disappointed.

With an investment philosophy, you always know how you will invest and why. You've factored in good markets and bad, and aren't swayed by hype or panic. Hope, gut instincts, and tips from your neighbor or cable financial news networks are not an investment philosophy. Instead, your investment philosophy should always do what it is supposed to, and it should be rational, defensible, and repeatable. No investment philosophy will work 100% of the time, but if your philosophy is prudent and evidence-based, chances are it will get you where you want to go over the long term.

Acknowledgments

It took the hard work, insights, and inspiration of many people to create this book. William Chettle handled much of the editing once all the stories were gathered. Not only did Dan Roam provide the superlative drawings, but he also helped us clarify and simplify our visual stories. Kate Tengberg brought her creative talents to the layout and cover design. Tom Zazueta helped lead the overall effort, while Cristina Yanez and Kelli Jelovic made invaluable editorial contributions and also helped keep everyone on track. We are especially grateful to everyone who provided us with stories and inspiration, particularly Alex Potts, David Booth, Ken French, Gene Fama, Gene Fama Jr., Ron Howard, Dan Wheeler, Rex Sinquefield, Randy Hardy, Mark Kalinowsky, Mark Fonville, Trey Nelson, Heather Hooper, Mike Nixon, Mike Ozburn, Ben Walker, Apollo Lupescu, Weston Wellington, Miye Wire, Darrel Smith, Joe Schildhauer, Chuck Vickery, Rob Ryan, John O'Neill, Paul Grace, Panch Romero, and many others including all of our colleagues that fully supported this book. Finally, we want to recognize all the independent financial advisors who provide comprehensive planning, backed by a prudent investment philosophy, to make a difference in the lives of their clients each and every day.

STEVEN J ATKINSON

Steven J. Atkinson, managing director of advisor relations at Buckingham Strategic Partners, has been helping investors and advisors become more informed for over 22 years. He has talked with investors from nearly every state and is always on the pursuit of uncovering the latest information and better ways to help families reach their goals. Steve holds the Certified Fund Specialist™ (CFS™) designation, is a co-author of "The Wealth Solution", and a frequent contributor to Buckingham's blog. He frequently speaks on behalf of wealth management firms across the country at client educational events. Steve lives in Omaha, Nebraska where he and his wife follow their three daughters as they pursue their soccer dreams.

DAN ROAM

Dan Roam is the author of five international bestselling books on business-visualization which have been translated into 31 languages. "The Back of the Napkin: Solving Problems with Pictures" was named by Fast Company, The London Times, and BusinessWeek as 'Creativity Book of the Year.' Dan's newest book, "Draw to Win" was just published by Penguin Portfolio and debuted as the #1 new book on amazon.com in the categories of Business Communications and Marketing & Sales. Dan has helped leaders at Google, Microsoft, Boeing, Gap, IBM, the U.S. Navy, the U.S. Senate, and the White House solve complex problems with simple pictures. Dan and his whiteboard appear frequently on CNN, MSNBC, ABC, CBS, Fox, and NPR.

[1] For illustrative purposes only and is not intended to represent actual portfolios or actual returns. Investing involves risk, including possible loss of principal.

[2] Indices are not available for direct investment. Their performance does not reflect the expenses associated with the management of an actual portfolio nor do indices represent results of actual trading. Information from sources deemed reliable, but its accuracy cannot be guaranteed. Performance is historical and does not guarantee future results. Total return includes reinvestment of dividends and capital gains.